EVERY DAY LEADERSHIP

SIMPLE AND UNCOMPLICATED EVERY DAY LEADERSHIP THOUGHTS

D. LANE STEPHENS

ISBN-13: 978-0-9832082-2-8

DEDICATION

.

Dedicated to all of those leaders who use their position power for good and not for evil

Introduction

I am sure that everyone reading this has read many books on leadership. There are many books about the subject and quite honestly, in my opinion, the vast majority of the books are never read cover to cover. Why not?

Many of the books are too wordy, too theoretical, and written by people who have degrees but not a lot of practical, day to day, hands-on leadership experience. People become bored reading theories on leadership.

People today also don't have that much time to read lengthy, wordy, abstract publications about leadership. They need to review information that is fast and easy to digest. They don't have hours to read. Life is too fast paced for that.

They do want to get better, to think, explore new ideas, and be reminded of ideas that they may already know but are not practicing. People also want to make sure what they do read adds value to their worlds.

I am not saying that all of those books were not of value. In every book I have read, I have taken away at least one idea that has helped me be better.

I have spent 37 years in the insurance business and have worked at something since I was 11. I have had the privilege of working for and with some great leaders, some good leaders, some awful leaders and some disastrous leaders. I have seen and observed leaders who should have never been allowed to be in a leadership role and observed some who were good leaders but not fully appreciated by their organizations because they were more effective at managing their people than managing up.

I have learned from every one of those leaders, including the bad ones. Even a bad leader can be a great example.

Theories and words on leadership can become boring. That is because Great Leaders are Great Leaders because of what they do every day. It is what you do everyday that counts.

Great Leaders are Great Leaders because of how they operate. Leadership is common sense and doing what your Mommas and your Daddies taught you growing up.

Leadership is not complicated. It is simple.

To some, these ideas will be a blinding glimpse of the obvious. Some of the information may even seem elementary or trivial to some of you, but as you will read, sometimes things work so well we stop doing them.

I hope that you can receive at least one idea or perhaps will be reminded of one idea that will help you be a better leader from this book. If you get at least that one idea, the time and money you have spent with this book will be worthwhile.

Every Day Leadership is set up to allow the reader to skip around and read the various thoughts. It can be kept around to serve as reminders of the day to day habits of leadership. Some of the ideas may seem redundant, but repetition helps us remember things better.

It is a quick read. I hope you enjoy and that you get at a minimum that one idea that can help you and your people.

D. Lane Stephens

ALWAYS, ALWAYS, ALWAYS, BE YOURSELF

You can't be something that you are not. Your people will see right through you and sense your insincerity. A person can fool someone for a short period of time, but on a day to day basis, you can't be something you are not. Your true character will always come out. Be yourself. Your people will respect you for who you are if you are true to yourself.

ALWAYS TELL THE TRUTH

Your people deserve the truth and so do you. Do you want your spouse or your children to lie to you? Of course you don't. Do you want one of your employees to lie to you? You base your decisions and your actions on the input you receive, so can you make the right decision if you are relying on false information? That is not likely.

Your people rely on you to tell them the truth. Their financial, emotional, and physical well-being is at stake. If you tell your people the truth, they will respond in kind and make decisions that will help you succeed. If you lie, they can't help you nor will they want to help you.

IF YOU HAVE SOLID CORE VALUES, THE TOUGH DECISIONS COME EASY

If you have solid core values, the tough decisions do come easy. It doesn't matter if it was your best rep that cheated. The decision is still the same no matter who cheated. You fire that rep immediately. You don't debate in your mind that this may be the biggest producer you have; you don't think about how much money you may lose. You fire the rep. If you don't, you are placing yourself and your organization in jeopardy. You gain the respect of the people in your organization and you don't waste time debating what you should do. The behavior of the rest of the organization will fall in line with the values of the organization as well since they see that you do not tolerate cheating.

NEVER, EVER PUT YOUR PEOPLE IN A POSITION WHERE THEY HAVE TO TELL A LITTLE STORY FOR YOU OR ANYONE ELSE

A common situation that is just as bad as lying yourself is placing your people in a position where they have to tell a little story for you or anyone else. If you are not taking calls then you are not available. You should never have your admin or anyone else communicate to folks that you are not in, if in fact, you are in. A lie is a lie and your people will feel that you have compromised them by putting them in that position. It isn't fair to your people to put them in that spot. It may seem like a small item or just a "little white lie", but a lie is still a lie and it makes your people uncomfortable. Make sure your people know you always tell the truth and they will model your behavior.

TREAT PEOPLE AS THEY WANT TO BE TREATED

People want to be noticed, they want to be respected, and they want to be rewarded for doing what they do. They want to know that you care about them and what happens to them. Treat them well and they will treat you well.

DELIVER NEWS TO PEOPLE WITHOUT PUTTING A SPIN ON THE NEWS

Your people will recognize a spin. You can help them see the positives, but never hide the negatives by putting a spin on the news. Spinning hurts your credibility and you will lose valuable time as your people discuss the spin rather than discuss the impacts of the news on the company and how to take advantage of the good news or how to overcome the bad news. The focus changes from the job on hand to the trust of the organization if you spin the news.

YOU HAVE PEOPLE WHO WORK WITH YOU, NOT FOR YOU

Always say that people work with you and not for you. It may not seem like much but it will mean a lot to the people you work with. It shows that you respect your people and that you don't consider them as just someone who does what you tell them to. It keeps you from coming off as arrogant and power hungry. If you truly feel that everyone in your organization works with you then everyone in the organization will work with you to take the organization to the levels you want. No one wants to just work at a job. They want to feel they are a part of something. This is one way of reinforcing that they are a "part of".

CARE ABOUT WHAT HAPPENS TO YOUR PEOPLE

People don't care as much as you think they do about how much you know. The want to know how much you care and you show that in what you do every day. You can't just tell them you care about them. You have to show it in how you operate every day and in your decisions. If you stop caring about your people, you are going to find it difficult to accomplish your organization's goal, because you are not going to have a lot of help in trying to get to the top.

YOUR ACTIONS SPEAK MUCH MORE LOUDLY THAN YOUR WORDS

What you do makes so much noise that people can't hear what you say. If you tell the organization that the organization will not tolerate harassment and you are having an affair with one of your employees, you will have zero credibility and your leadership will always be questioned. If you tell your people that you want a diverse organization and everyone that reports to you is of your race and gender, the fact that you do not have diversity within your own immediate team speaks more loudly than your words. If you have an Ethics Policy and then you ask your financial people to go back and recalculate the earnings for the quarter and tell them to make sure they meet the expectations, your actions are not matching what you say or publish. Your credibility will be destroyed.

WALK THE TALK

Walking the talk is just being who you say you are and doing what you say you are going to do. If you tell your people that it is important to work hard and you come in late, leave early, and goof off most of the day, you are not walking the talk. If you tell your people to work hard, then you need to walk the talk by being right there with them, working even harder than they do. If you tell them not to lie and then you have your admin tell people who call that you are not in when you are actually in, you are not walking the talk.

LISTEN TO YOUR PEOPLE

You need to stay in touch with your people and know what is going on with them, your organization, and your customers. They know what they need to be able to do their jobs better; they know what the customers need; they know what the organization needs. Ask them to help you. They will. They will tell you how they feel if they believe that you are actually listening and hearing them. They will take your organization to the levels you want to attain if you listen.

SMILING IS GOOD FOR YOUR LEADERSHIP

A smile is contagious. A smile says you are warm, you are approachable and that you are happy. It says you are open. If you smile, so will your people. If your people are smiling, your customers will smile. If your customers are smiling, they will tell other people how good you are and the increased sales and profits will continue to help you smile. Smile a lot.

HAVE AN ATTITUDE OF GRATITUDE

Always remember that things could be worse and that for others it is. You need to remember that sales and profit don't just come in the door. They come in the door because you have something to offer. You should be grateful that for whatever the reason, you have something to offer.

Your people could work somewhere else and without the efforts of your people you will not have happy customers nor make much money. Be grateful that they have chosen to work with you and that they are trying to help you build your business or your career.

ALWAYS KEEP YOUR PEOPLE INFORMED

The news and information is being passed around any way, and people are putting their spin on things. Better that they hear the information from you than from others. You can calm fears, eliminate misconceptions and minimize the distractions in your organization if you will tell your people what is going on all the time.

LET YOUR PEOPLE KNOW YOUR VISION OF WHERE THE ORGANIZATION IS GOING

Your people will help you take the organization where you want it to go if they know where you want it to go. They will make their decisions with that thought in mind. If they don't know, your organization will be confused and people will try to read your mind as to where you want it to go. Your organization will flounder without that vision.

RECOGNIZE PEOPLE FOR DOING GOOD THINGS

For many people, being recognized for their efforts and their accomplishments means just as much as money. In interviews, I ask the question which motivates you more, "Pay, prestige, accomplishments or recognition," and recognition came up just as often as the others. Everyone wants to feel appreciated and that you have noticed that they are doing a good job. Notice your people, recognize them, and reward them and they will walk through walls for you!

ALLOW FOR MISTAKES AS THE ONLY PEOPLE NOT MAKING MISTAKES ARE THOSE WHO ARE NOT DOING ANYTHING

You want to encourage people to take risks, to stretch themselves and elevate their performance to the highest levels possible. That is not going to happen if they feel that you are going to chastise them or fire them for making a mistake. They will not be able to perform at peak performance level if they are doing everything they can to avoid a mistake. It will mean they are not going out of their way to take on more if all they can do perfectly is what they normally do. Allow for mistakes. It is how we learn. If someone never makes a mistake it is because they are not working up to their potential.

LET PEOPLE DO THEIR JOBS... THE WHOLE JOB

The worst thing you can do is assign a task to someone but keep stepping in and doing it for them. Let them do the whole job so that they can feel the accomplishment of finishing the task. If you jump back in on an assignment and take it over, it shows that you have no confidence in the individual. They will not grow and they will always be looking to you for guidance. You will wear yourself out and spend your time doing things that someone else should be doing. You will not be able to multiply yourself and your organization if you are trying to do everything. Make them give you scheduled updates along the way to make sure they are on track and to provide coaching if necessary, but don't take the task away from them.

NEVER ASK ANYONE TO DO ANYTHING THAT YOU WOULD NOT DO YOURSELF

You should never put your people in a position that you would not willingly go into yourself. It is not fair and it shows a lack of respect for the individual if you would never do what you have asked the person to do. It shows that you do not value them as individuals. You will lose your credibility if you ask them to do something you would not do yourself.

CORRECT THE BEHAVIOR, NOT THE PERSON

It isn't the person that needs to be corrected; it is the behavior they are demonstrating. You want people to feel that you value them, care for them and respect them.   If you belittle them individually, they will certainly not feel that you value them. You can't change people, but you can change their behavior.

WHEN ADDRESSING A PERFORMANCE PROBLEM, DO IT IN PRIVATE

Never criticize someone in public. Always address performance issues privately. You must always leave a person's dignity intact and private performance discussions are healthy and necessary to do that. If you criticize someone publicly not only do you embarrass the individual, you also lose credibility with the rest of the organization. You will lose their respect. When you address a performance problem, you want the result to be a correction of the behavior and improved results. You don't want the result to be an employee or employees who are angry and resentful.

NEVER TAKE AWAY ANYONE'S DIGNITY

If you take way someone's dignity, nothing good can happen. It hurts them and it hurts you. You want people who feel good about themselves and about you. You have an impact on people and you need to think about how you talk to and about people. Never take away someone's dignity.

ACTIVATE THE BRAIN BEFORE ACTIVATING THE MOUTH

You should not be hearing what you are saying at the same time every body else hears it. What you say has an impact and if you are speaking before you think about it, there is no telling what you may be saying. We all learned that if you don't have anything to say, don't speak, but talking before you think about the audience and the impact of your words, is just as important if not more so.

REMEMBER TO LAUGH A LOT EVERYDAY

Laughter keeps us young, it keeps us loose and it allows us to put things in perspective. People want to work in places where it is fun and challenging. If you laugh a lot everyday, your people will want to be there with you. Laughter allows us to deal with the stress and to give our work our best shots. If your people are laughing and having a good time, so will your customers.

LAUGH AT YOURSELF

Don't take yourself so seriously. Your people need to realize that you know you are human and that you make mistakes. Demonstrate some humility. Laugh at what you do. You will live longer and your people will respect you more, not less.

BE OUT AND ABOUT

The only way to know what is going on in your organization is to be out with them. You learn a lot about what is going on and it gives you a chance to recognize people by catching them doing something right. It also helps you to learn what needs to be improved because your people will feel comfortable showing you if you are out there with them. Chances are good that they will never come into your office and tell you that something needs to be improved but they will tell you if you are out there with them. They will also know that you care if you are with them and not closed off somewhere.

BE EXCITED AND ENERGETIC!!!!!

If you are excited and energetic, your people will be as well. Excited and energetic people accomplish a lot more than those who are not. If you are excited and enthusiastic then the atmosphere will be lively and fun and exciting! It will be a place where people want to perform!

CREATE AN ENVIRONMENT WHERE YOUR PEOPLE FEEL SAFE AND SECURE

It is critical that your people feel that they can perform their tasks without worrying about their physical or emotional security. No one should feel that their personal safety is jeopardized at work. Make sure that no one is trying to intimidate them or make them feel uncomfortable with sexual innuendo, advances or discrimination. Make sure that no one is viewing, or posting inappropriate material. Make sure that racism or bigotry is not tolerated in your organization.

CREATE AN ENVIRONMENT WHERE PEOPLE WANT TO BE

You want your people to enjoy coming to work every day! It's not that difficult. Hire good people. Make sure they have the tools they need. Make sure they know where you want the organization to go and make sure that you celebrate the good things you accomplish along the way. Laugh and keep the atmosphere light but one that is high-charged. As the leader, your people will emulate your behavior. Be someone that they want to be like. Tell them you appreciate them and what they do. Recognize them and reward them. Most of all care for them.

ASK PEOPLE FOR THEIR SUGGESTIONS, THEIR OPINIONS, AND THEIR CRITIQUE

No one has all of the answers. No one can keep up with all of the information that comes our way. We need people to review what we are doing to make sure we haven't missed anything and that we are on the right path. We sometimes get so close to the forest that we can't see the trees. We need someone to tell us that and we need to listen. Get rid of the arrogance and realize that you don't have all of the answers. Your people and you together may have all of the answers.

DON'T SHOOT THE MESSENGER

If someone brings you news you don't want to hear, you should not be angry with them and do what is commonly called "Shoot the Messenger." If you shoot the messenger, no one will bring you any news other than what they think will be good news for you. You will shut down the organization if you start shooting the messenger.

DO WHAT YOUR MOMMAS & DADDIES TAUGHT YOU

Do the things that your Mommas and your Daddies taught you when you were 5. Share, respect, have manners, say please and thank you, etc, etc, etc. Those lessons still mean a lot in how effectively you work with your people, your vendors and your customers.

WHEN YOU MAKE A MISTAKE... ADMIT IT, APOLOGIZE, AND LEARN FROM IT

Don't deflect a mistake, make excuses, or blame it on any one else. The people in your organization will lose respect for you if you do. Your customers, your suppliers, your people will all look past a mistake if you admit and apologize for it. If you don't, they will remember that mistake. It is also very important to learn from your mistakes in order to prevent them from happening again if you can.

DO BUSINESS THE RIGHT WAY

When you do business the right way, you feel better, you sleep better, and you can face yourself in the mirror. You also establish valuable lifetime customers as people want to continue doing business with you and will also tell others about the way you do business. Do business the right way...the way you want someone to do business with you.

THE END RESULT NEVER JUSTIFIES THE MEANS IF THE MEANS WERE INAPPROPRIATE

The end result never justifies the means. A win at any cost attitude may work for a brief period of time but it will not allow you to build a long term business and long term relationships. Cutting corners, cheating, telling white lies, misleading people, not revealing the whole truth catches up with you. How you get to the end result does matter.

A HALF-TRUTH IS STILL DISHONEST

If you only tell half of the story and not the whole story it is still dishonest. For example, telling someone that the used car they want to buy starts every time without telling them after two miles it runs hot and it can't be fixed is withholding information and a lie. You told a half-truth but not the whole truth. Withholding valuable information is wrong. Tell the whole truth.

BEING LEGALLY TRUTHFULL IS NOT THE SAME AS BEING HONEST

Be honest. Don't play games. Tell the truth. When your sales contract says "After leaving the Arizona State University College of Architecture, I began designing homes" people think you graduated as an Architect. What it doesn't say is that you only went to the bathroom there or walked down the hallway, then started designing homes. Legally, the claim isn't a lie and is legally truthful but it is not the same as being honest. There is a big difference between legally truthful and being honest.

IF YOU EVER ASK YOURSELF, "WILL I GET CAUGHT?" YOU OBVIOUSLY SHOULD NOT DO WHAT YOU ARE CONTEMPLATING

I can tell you the answer is yes no matter what and you should not do what you are contemplating. You will have to face the mirror and you will always know what you have done even if you don't get caught. You will get caught though, trust me, and you should never put yourself in that spot.

YOUR PEOPLE WILL BE WATCHING HOW YOU HANDLE ISSUES

If your best sales rep cheats in order to make a sale or win a contest, the organization is going to watch how you handle it. If you try to ignore it, make excuses for the individual, or issue temporary discipline, you will lose all credibility with your people. What you do will speak so much more loudly than what you say and this is a tremendous opportunity to walk the talk and to be the person you say you are. If you want an organization that does business the right way, tells the truth and makes sure any headlines generated are positive ones, fire the rep. There is no gray here. Whether it is your best rep or your worst rep, you fire them. The rest of the organization will take notice and make sure they are doing business the right way and they will respect you. With that respect, you get great results that are real.

IF YOU HAVE SOMEONE WITH A PERFORMANCE ISSUE, DEAL WITH IT QUICKLY

Your performance standard is the standard set by your lowest performing employee.   If you do not correct the performance issues, then you are saying to the rest of the organization, this performance is OK and I am willing to continue paying someone for this level of performance. On the other hand, if you deal with the performance issue quickly then people realize that the organization has high expectations and that no one is going to drag the organization down.   Their performance will rise to the appropriate levels.

ENCOURAGE YOUR PEOPLE TO GROW

The reality is that you are either growing or you are dying because if you are not growing then you are just getting older. Encourage your people to grow. They will appreciate your wanting them to challenge themselves and to learn new things. That is a real key to keeping excited, enthusiastic, motivated people performing at a high level. If they are not growing they get bored and with boredom they become complacent. If your people are bored, you can bet your customers will be as well. If your people don't grow, your competitors will grow right by you and your business could die. You need growing people to grow your company and your profits.

ENCOURAGE YOUR PEOPLE TO DEVELOP THEIR WHOLE BEING

Don't just encourage personal development that helps them do their jobs. Encourage personal development that helps them develop their whole being. Encourage them to grow spiritually, physically, mentally and emotionally. Well-rounded, balanced people will be more productive and they will live longer. They will also be a lot more fun to work with. If someone gets all of their rewards in one area of their life, if something goes wrong in that area, it can be devastating to the individual. Make sure that people develop in all areas of their lives.

HAVE THE COURAGE NECESSARY TO STAND BY YOUR CONVICTIONS

It isn't always easy to do but it is one of the keys to being that person you say you are. If you think smoking is dangerous and kills people, then you shouldn't sell cigarettes. If you think that crediting sales or profits in a different quarter in order to make the results look better is wrong, do not do it and do not work for an organization that requires you to do that.

Having courage to stand by your convictions means that even if the decision you have to make to stay true to your convictions costs you your job or a lot of money, you still make that decision. You will win in the long run if you stand by your convictions.

BE THE SAME PERSON INSIDE AND OUTSIDE THE WORKPLACE

If you are different outside the workplace, then you probably are not who you say you are inside the workplace. You cannot be someone you are not and be an effective leader. One of the keys to being a great leader is to be genuine and real. You can't be that if you are different with your family and your friends than with the people who work with you.

WHEN MEETING WITH YOUR PEOPLE, LISTEN TO EVERYONE'S IDEAS WITHOUT JUDGING THEM OR MAKING FUN OF ANYONE'S IDEAS

When Colonel Sanders of Kentucky Fried Chicken suggested that they knock a hole in the walls of their buildings in order to hand the chicken to people in the cars, there was probably someone in that room laughing. If the leaders of that organization laughed at that suggestion, it may have taken a while for the drive through to be created for KFC to really make their fast food chicken really fast for the consumer.   How about the employee sitting in the room who said let's sell bottled water when everyone has access to tap water that is really cheap? Do you think she may have been laughed at if that is how that happened?

The people who work with you in your organization are the ones who can come up with ideas that will make your business better. If you or the leaders of the organization laugh or make fun of someone's ideas, you will shut the rest of the organization down, and the only ideas you will get are the safe ones that most people think best matches your views.

RESPOND TO EVERY QUESTION ASKED AND NEVER LET ANYONE FEEL THAT YOU THOUGHT THEIR QUESTION WAS STUPID

When you are meeting with your people, you need to make sure that you catch every question and answer each question. It takes courage for people to ask questions or make comments in front of a group so the effective leader acknowledges people for having that courage. It shows respect to the individual and lets him or her know that they are important to the organization.

You can learn a lot about your organization by the questions you get. You will know if the communication process is working in your organization and if everyone is on the same page. You will be able to learn who the group looks to for leadership among themselves and you will learn which groups or teams have ineffective leadership. One can learn as much by the types of questions people ask as listening to others present or share.

If you make people feel their question was stupid, you will not learn valuable information and you will shut the organization down.

DON'T RESPOND TO A QUESTION BY SAYING THAT'S A GOOD QUESTION

If you are not saying that to each question asked, then some people with think their question wasn't a good one since you did not tell them "That's a good question." Make it all or none or you will leave people doubting themselves again. They will be less willing to take a risk and ask a question in the future.

BE WILLING TO NOT DO BUSINESS WITH SOMEONE IF YOU FEEL THEY ARE NOT HONEST AND DON'T OPERATE WITH INTEGRITY

You will send the wrong message to your people if you do business with that person or that entity. As your momma and daddy used to try to teach you, you are known by the company you keep. If you sleep with big dogs, you get big fleas. It is just a matter of time that doing business with a company that doesn't operate with integrity gives you issues that will test your own integrity and principles. Your people know who the shady ones are and how they operate. Don't put your people in positions where they have to deal with people and organizations that compromise ethical and perhaps legal considerations.

BE WILLING TO WALK AWAY FROM A SALE OR A DEAL IF IT'S GOING TO COMPROMISE YOUR VALUES...
AND ACTUALLY WALK AWAY

Again, be who you say you are. Stay true to your convictions. It may cost you some money in the short term but in the long run, you win. You will have the respect of your organization and you don't have to look over your shoulder. You can also look at yourself in the mirror a lot easier.

DO NOT TOLERATE HARRASSMENT ANYWHERE IN YOUR OPERATION (Part 1)

Your people should be able to work in an environment where they feel safe and welcome. If you have an individual who harasses another associate, you need to deal with that immediately. Your people will know who you are by how you deal with these types of issues. If you look the other way, or cover the behavior up for the harassing employee, not only do you have a good chance of facing litigation, you will also lose the respect of your people. Do not let an individual, no matter how valuable their performance, harass another individual.

DO NOT TOLERATE HARRASSMENT ANYWHERE IN YOUR OPERATION (Part 2)

You need to be proactive to insure that if harassment is being reported to others in the organization that are close to you, that they are dealing with that behavior immediately. You have to make sure they are not looking the other way. The rest of the organization will assume that you know what is going on and will think you are not dealing with the behavior. Make sure that the organization knows it is OK to report harassing behavior to a level above their immediate supervisor and all the way to you as the head of the organization. They need to feel that it is safe to do that.

DO NOT TOLERATE BIAS AND/OR DISCRIMINATION IN YOUR OPERATION

Not only are all of these illegal, it would just be wrong and bad business practice to tolerate this type of behavior. The world today is diverse and complex with a merging of different cultures. Your organization needs to be just like our society today; made up of people from different cultures, backgrounds, ages, sexes, and races. It is the only way to know what your different customers prefer and it is also the right thing to do.

You must do everything you can to prevent bias and/or discrimination in your organization. If you discover it, deal with it immediately.

HIRE PEOPLE YOU ARE WILLING TO TAKE HOME TO MEET YOUR FAMILY

You want an organization that reflects good values, ethics, principles, and does business the right way. You can only accomplish that by hiring people who operate that way. If you ask yourself, would I have this person in my home to meet my family and the answer is yes, you probably have a good match. If the answer is no, don't hire them.

BE CAREFUL OF THE TO-DO LIST MENTALITY

Keeping a To Do List allows you to stay on top of things and to make sure you utilize your time effectively. Just make sure that you don't develop a To Do List Mentality where you see how many of the items you can get off that list each day. Make sure that you are utilizing the To Do List to do the High Payoff Priority Items on that list first. It truly is quality rather than quantity that counts for the leader. You can relieve a lot of stress by scratching through items on that list as complete, but it may not get you to where you want to go with your business.

THE DIFFERENTIAL FOR SUCCESSFUL PEOPLE IS THE ABILITY TO GET THE JOB DONE, NO MATTER WHAT OBSTACLES COME THEIR WAY

This is absolutely true for the leader. No matter what the obstacles, the great leaders find a way to get the job done. That is what differentiates the great leaders from the adequate ones. Any one can lead when things are smooth and calm. However, our lives and our initiatives don't always go smoothly.   There are external issues that impact us that we can't control. We can only control how we react to them. The great leaders recognize that they are where they are because they get the job done. No matter what, they get the job done.

BE PROACTIVE, NOT REACTIVE

It is always the proactive items that will make you successful. You have to react but if you are always reacting, you are standing in place and just running an existing business. You are pretty much just trying to survive. If you are not proactive, you are not growing and expanding and finding ways to get better. You are not thinking your way through where you want to go and how you will get there. You are in sports terminology "back on your heels" and trying to avoid getting scored on. Call the plays that will help you grow and score. Put someone else in the reactive mode. You will ultimately drive them out of your business.

KEEP AN OFFENSIVE TO DO LIST AND A DEFENSIVE TO DO LIST

The biggest reason you keep two lists is to make sure that you do remain proactive and that you don't just react and play defense all day. You have to be on the offense to score in most sports and the same is true in business. If you spend all of your time doing all of those defensive items, then you will not get on the offense. If the other team has the ball more than you and you are trying to avoid them scoring then you are not going to score yourself. Make sure that you spend the right amount of time on the offense.

BEWARE OF THE TYRANNY OF THE URGENT...BE PROACTIVE AND ON THE OFFENSE

It is easy to let the "pink slips" overwhelm you. Those are those phone messages that keep piling up on your desk and in your voice mail. That is the tyranny of the urgent. Someone needs you right now or you have a problem that needs to be solved right now. The tyranny of the urgent can keep you from being on the offense and being proactive. Avoid that at all costs.

ANYONE CAN HAVE A GOOD YEAR WHEN THE BUSINESS CLIMATE IS GOOD... THE REAL LEADERS HAVE GOOD YEARS NO MATTER WHAT THE BUSINESS CLIMATE

When the economy is good and the business climate is good, anyone can have a good year and do good things. It is easy to plan, easy to execute the strategy, and usually there are no surprises that require contingency plans.   The great leaders find ways to have great years even when the climate is bad. They know it is more difficult to plan, more difficult to implement and execute, and there are surprises almost every day.   They find ways around and through the problems and get the job done. Their ability to have a good year no matter what external issues are at play is what makes them great leaders. They lift organizations to great achievements no matter what the business climate.

UNDER PROMISE AND OVER DELIVER AND NOT THE REVERSE!!!

It is so much easier to get something done earlier and better than you promised rather than get something done later and/or worse than you promised. In our desire to please, sometimes we promise more than we can deliver. It is far better to set the right expectations up front and then do better than that!

OPERATE UNDER THE KISS THEORY...KEEP IT SIMPLE AND STRAIGHT FORWARD!

The most effective leaders operate under the Kiss Theory. They Keep it Simple and Straightforward. Effective leaders do not complicate things. They know there are a few key items that have to be done right every day and they do not complicate their businesses with unnecessary items. The more complicated your processes and your plans, the easier it is for mistakes to occur. It also confuses your people, and they end up trying to do too many things or doing the things they are supposed to do incorrectly. Don't confuse your customers, your people, or yourself. Just keep it simple and straightforward!

THE MOST SUCCESSFUL PEOPLE ARE USUALLY THE EASIEST TO DEAL WITH

The most successful people have inner confidence and less need to utilize power plays or intimidation to let you know how important they are. They are at peace with themselves and what they do. They are usually the ones who go out of their way to make you feel comfortable and to answer your questions. They will be more willing to share with you how they do things. To be the most effective leader you need to be easy to deal with. Get your ego out of the way and don't continually do things to remind them that you are the boss. If you are an effective leader they will know you are the head of the organization and they will not resent you for it. Be easy to deal with. Demand exceptional performance and results but be easy to deal with.

THERE IS NEVER ENOUGH TIME TO DO IT RIGHT THE FIRST TIME, BUT IT SEEMS THERE IS ALWAYS TIME TO DO IT OVER...DO IT RIGHT THE FIRST TIME!

A little extra time up front saves you a lot of time in the long run if you do things right the first time. If you are spending your time re-doing things, then you are not spending your time on proactive items. You waste money as well as time if you have to do anything over again. Do it right the first time.

DO THE RIGHT THINGS RIGHT AND AT THE RIGHT TIME!

Just doing things right isn't going to make your organization successful. You have to make sure you are doing the right things right. Your timing has to be good as well in order to capitalize on opportunities when they present themselves. Great leaders not only do things right, they also do the right things and at that right time.

CHARACTER-DO NOT LEAVE HOME WITHOUT IT!!!!

This is just another way of saying that you need to do business the right way, ethically and honestly. It says that whoever you are and whatever your values, don't leave them at home. Take them where ever you go.

NO MATTER HOW HARD YOU TRY, YOU CAN'T TEACH A DUCK TO CHACE MICE!!!!!!!!!!

If you need to catch mice, you can't hire a bunch of ducks and teach them to catch mice. You need cats that instinctively catch mice. While you can teach people to do a lot of things, you have to make sure that the roles they are playing are a good fit for them. If you need someone to run a marathon, you don't recruit the 100 meter dash person. You recruit someone with the ability to run the marathon or to have the mental discipline necessary to learn the training regimen necessary to be able to run a marathon. If you need cats, don't hire ducks.

DON'T JUST WANT TO DO BETTER, BE WILLING TO BE BETTER!!!

Everyone wants to have a better year, be more successful, make more money, but not every body wants to be better. The real key is to want to be better. Just wanting to do better may mean that you are just hoping or wishing for a lucky break or your boss gives you a raise. If you want to be better, and take the steps to be better, you will do better. Want to be better, not just do better.

WATCH OUT FOR THE PEOPLE WITH PERMANENT POTENTIAL...THE WORLD IS FULL OF THEM

The world is full of people with permanent potential. I am sure you know the type. They have the intelligence, they have the knowledge, they look the part and every one expects them to succeed. You hear over and over again, that person has potential. However, many people never apply themselves and get to the level of success that one would expect them to attain given their tools. They have permanent potential because they don't apply that potential to their roles or the companies they work with. They never reach the level of success they could reach. When you look for people to work with you beware of these people. Find people who have found ways to get the job done and get the results necessary. Find the ones who can apply their skills to get the needed results. Avoid the people with permanent potential.

AS A LEADER YOU CAN'T AFFORD TO CONFUSE THE "OUGHTABE'S" WITH THE REALITIES!

Many people confuse the "oughtabe's" with the realities. The business climate ought to be better. Finding the right people ought to be easy. In reality, the business climate is sometimes not good. In reality, finding good people can be difficult. As the leader, you must be grounded in the realities of the world in which you operate. You can think about how you can make the "oughtabe's" realities, but realize you need to be able to know the difference.

YOU CAN'T SELL IT IF YOU DON'T TELL IT. NO MATTER HOW GOOD YOUR PRODUCT OR YOUR PRESENTATION, IF YOU DON'T TELL IT TO SOMEONE, YOU CAN'T SELL IT!!!!!!!

As a leader, one of your key responsibilities is to communicate your vision and your plans to attain that vision to your people. You need to be in front of your people as often as you can continually talking about the organization and where it is headed. Additionally, you need to be in front of your customers selling what you can do for them and in front of potential investors and stockholders. No matter how good you are, how good your product or service is, if you don't tell the story often and well, you will not be successful. Tell your story often and to a lot of people.

FOCUS ON WHAT YOU CAN CONTROL WHILE ANTICIPATING AND BEING PREPARED FOR WHAT YOU DON'T CONTROL

Execute your game plan everyday doing the very best you can, taking care of your people and your customers. Execution of your strategy is in your control. At the same time you need to anticipate actions by external competitors and entities (government) that could have an impact on your business and be prepared to react to those external circumstances. Have contingency plans in place if external forces dictate a change in strategy.

BE A VISIBLE LEADER

You need to be visible to your employees, your customers and all stakeholders of your organization. They all need to see that you are engaged and that you are there for them.

IF THE AGREEMENT IS ONLY IN AIR, YOU HAVEN'T A PRAYER

We should still be able to shake hands with someone and know that they will live up to their end of the agreement. Unfortunately, there are unethical and dishonest people and companies around. There are also people and companies whose circumstances change and they may not honor your agreements. You have to get things in writing with confirmations from the other party as to what they agreed to. If you don't have it in writing, then all you have is air and that means you haven't a prayer of getting something resolved if it goes awry.

THE BIG PRINT GIVETH, THE SMALL PRINT TAKETH AWAY

Unfortunately there are companies and individuals who feel it is OK to place the important "Gotcha" items or the more controversial items in small print. Always read the contracts you sign. The big print doesn't always reveal the key items you need to know.

REMEMBER THAT PEOPLE READ THE WHITE PRINT

Some people spend their time reading the white lines in the communication. In other words they read things that aren't there between the lines. With key communications, it pays to have conversations as well as written communication in order to make sure that there are no misconceptions that will distract the people in your organization. Have open discussions and dialogues. Also, with some communications, have people send you an email or a note with what they understand the communication says. That will insure that they are hearing and reading what you intended the message to convey.

LEADING IS NOT A SPECTATOR SPORT

You can't just watch what is happening in your organization and be the leader. You have to be engaged and involved.

HAVING A DIVERSE ENVIRONMENT IN YOUR ORGANIZATION IS NOT ROCKET SCIENCE

Creating a diverse environment isn't rocket science. It isn't having committees on diversity, training on the need for diversity, or structured programs. It is making sure you have an organization that realizes they don't know all of the answers and values differing opinions. It is making sure your organization listens to all employees, respects everyone and seeks out diverse people in the recruiting process.

WHEN DEALING WITH PERFORMANCE ISSUES, THE DREAD IS ALWAYS WORSE THAN THE DOING

We always expect the worst. If you dread dealing with poor performance, you procrastinate and the performance does not get better. It normally gets worse. You will find that the dread of dealing with the performance is always worse than actually dealing with it. In almost every termination due to poor performance, the people end up better off as does the organization. Many people are actually relieved and they can find a role that will be a better fit for them. The actual discussions and the terminations are never as bad as the dread we feel prior to the discussion or termination.

YOU ARE EITHER GROWING OR YOU ARE DYING

If you aren't growing then all you are doing is getting older and that much closer to death. Take responsibility for your own growth as organizations and life will grow right past you if you don't. Think about it...your grandparents did not need to know how to operate a computer to be successful and to do their jobs. Now it is hard to find a job that doesn't require some level of basic computer skills. New technology and products are developing every day. Keep learning and growing.

THE PACE OF CHANGE IS SUCH THAT IF YOU DON'T TAKE ACCOUNTABILITY FOR YOUR PERSONAL GROWTH, THE ORGANIZATION WILL GROW RIGHT PAST YOU

I have seen many individuals who were considered stars and leaders in organizations that just kept doing the same thing every day and as a result were left behind. The individuals allowed their efforts to focus only on today's results and left themselves vulnerable to change requiring new skills. Do not let that happen to you or to the people you lead. Insure continuous learning in your organization.

YOU MUST HAVE PROFITABLE GROWTH...NO COMPANY DIETS OR TRIMS THEIR WAY TO GREATNESS

Right sizing or down sizing may bring short term relief and results but the only way to be a great company is to have profitable revenue growth. Shrinking your number of employees will only make your company more valuable and great long term if the productivity improves and you find a way to grow with the fewer employees. The measure of greatness is still growth.

YOUR SALES PEOPLE DON'T SELL ANYONE ANYTHING; THEY HELP THEM BUY SOMETHING THE CLIENT WANTS OR NEEDS!!!!

No one wants to hear that they were sold anything or that someone else was sold something. That has a negative connotation. Great sales people help people buy something they need or want. As the leader, make sure your people have that nuance down pat. Don't let them say they sold anything. They make sales because they helped the customer buy what they needed.

WE HAVE A TENDENCY TO GO HUNTING WITH AN ELEPHANT GUN, BUT IT IS USUALLY THE MOSQUITO'S THAT ARE BITING OUR REAR ENDS!!!

Good leaders realize that the productivity drain is not from the big challenges that come to their organizations. It is a lot of little issues that drain organizations. Little issues that multiply and become big issues. Too many organizations set plans in place to protect themselves from the elephants while the little mosquitoes destroy them because the weapons to defeat the elephants won't work with the mosquitoes.

LACK OF PLANNING BY LEADERS SHOULD NOT CONSTITUTE AN EMERGENCY FOR THE ORGANIZATION

Many leaders wait until the last minute and do not plan their times for items that need to get done. They then create emergencies for the rest of the organization to meet deadlines and/or to win business. Don't create emergencies for others because you waited to ask for help or didn't plan appropriately.

IF IT WALKS LIKE A DUCK AND QUACKS LIKE A DUCK, IT MUST BE A DUCK

Quite simply, call it like it is. Don't try to make a situation something it isn't. Good leaders call it like it is.

REMEMBER IT IS READY, AIM, FIRE AND NOT FIRE, READY, AIM

Many people who are in leadership roles make this mistake. They take action without being ready to take action. They shoot the arrow, miss the target because they were not ready and then move their target to where the arrow stuck. They justify their actions by indicating that they hit the target but it was only after the target was moved. The best leaders get ready by knowing where the target is and what it is going to take to hit it, take steps to get in position to hit the target, and then shoot. They usually hit the target.

HOPE IS NOT A STRATEGY

Many times you find people in leadership positions who really do not have a strategy to attain their goals. In effect, they are operating with the Hope Strategy. I hope our actions will help us hit our goals. I hope that we do the things necessary to get there. You do provide hope for your people if you have a strategy that will enable you to hit your goals. Hope is not a strategy. It will not make you successful on its own.

GUARD AGAINST INSANITY

The definition of insanity is doing the same thing over and over again expecting different results. If your practices and actions are not working, then don't keep doing them over and over and expect that they will work. For some reason, we are just like the alcoholic who tries to drink again. This time it will be different the alcoholic thinks as he or she takes a drink. It will not be different. You will get the same results.

LOOK PEOPLE IN THE EYE!!!!

Always make eye contact. People think that people who don't make eye contact are trying to hide something. They don't assume you are shy or are busy. They assume you are hiding something. Making eye contact says you are acknowledging people, you are listening to them, you respect them, and you are shooting straight with them. Don't look away. Look people in the eye.

NEVER FOLD YOUR ARMS

When you are talking or listening, never fold your arms. It tells people you are either defensive or you are not open to any other opinion other than your own. It shuts down conversations. What you do says so much more than what you say and people will instantly know if you are being defensive or inflexible if your arms are folded.

SAY PLEASE AND THANK YOU TO EVERYONE...YOUR CUSTOMERS, YOUR SUPPLIERS, YOUR BOSSES, YOUR COLLEAGUES, YOUR PEOPLE...EVERYONE

Saying please and thank you is a sign of respect and that you appreciate the things people do for you. It is the right thing to do. If you keep asking people to do things for you and you do not say please nor thank you when they have done them, people may not want to do those for you again. You may be the boss and not feel that you have to say please or thank you. You may think that your people should do the things you ask them to do. They will. However, their enthusiasm to do the task and the results you receive will be a lot better if you say please and thank you. Keep in mind it isn't the big production or event that says look what I am doing for you. It is what you do everyday that counts and makes a difference. It is truly all of what seems like the little things, but they are really the big things that cost so little and take such little time.

TREAT EVERYONE WITH RESPECT

It does not matter who it is, everyone deserves your respect. Your higher power did not create any junk. Always pay attention to the people who are truly successful and viewed as great leaders. They treat everyone they meet equally and with respect. That means your customers, all levels of people you work with, your vendors, your family...everyone! Take a lesson from how prospective spouses, prospective employers and prospective customers make decisions on their future mates, future employers and future suppliers. They watch how you treat the waiters or the waitresses. Everyone has dreams, they have value, and they are important. Treat them with respect.

YOUR STANDARD OF PERFORMANCE BECOMES THE WEAKEST PERFORMER IN YOUR ORGANIZATION

Your standard of performance becomes your weakest performer. That individual's performance tells the organization the level of performance you are willing to accept. Always raise the bar of your weakest performers or you need to help them find the career that best fits them. If you don't, you run the risk of some of your people performing less than they are capable of performing.

BE ON TIME
ALWAYS...ALWAYS...ALWAYS!!!!

It is disrespectful to be late to a meeting or an appointment. It sends a message that something or someone else was more important. Sometimes it can't be helped and for those times, an apology is in order for the people who were inconvenienced by your being late. Being late also sends a message that you could be disorganized or scattered or overwhelmed. It is never OK to be fashionably late. Good leaders are always on time and expect their people to do likewise.

ACTIVELY LISTEN TO FOLKS!!!!!

Be in the moment. Put down the pen, turn away from the laptop. Look at people when they speak to you. Hear what they are saying. Acknowledge what they are saying. Too many people have no idea what someone just said to them because they were mentally someplace else. People always know if you are not really listening to them.

COOPERATE WITH COLLEAGUES AND OTHERS

Everyone can help you and everyone can hurt you. Many organizations spend more of their time on internal barriers and turf wars than on external barriers and opportunities. An organization cooperating with each other for the good of the organization will be so much better than those fighting and sabotaging each other.

DO NOT HIRE FROM A CANDIDATE POOL OF ONE

When you are recruiting or hiring, if you only have a candidate pool of one, the candidate will almost always seem like a good selection. Always have enough people in your candidate pool to be able to do a comparison. Good talent makes us good leaders. If you make a mistake in the hiring process you lose money and time. You can lose your business. Hiring from a pool of one means you better be lucky. More times than not, you will not be lucky.

A SUCCESSFUL TRACK RECORD IS THE BEST PREDICTER OF FUTURE SUCCESS

It is easy for people to tell you how good they are and what they will accomplish. Dig into their backgrounds. Were they successful in their previous roles?   In college? In high school? If people were successful previously, chances are good they will be successful again.

ALLOW PEOPLE YOU ARE INTERVIEWING TO GET TO KNOW YOU AND YOUR ORGANIZATION

What you don't want to happen is for someone you have hired to come to you and say this isn't what I thought I was getting into when I came to work here. The interview process should not just be for you. It should be for the candidate as well. You want them to know the organization as much as they can. They need to know if they are a fit with the culture. Turnover costs money and time and can cost you your business. Make sure they get to know your company and the people. If your company is well led, you will want them to know all they can.

EVERY DECISION YOU MAKE SHOULD PASS THE FRONT PAGE TEST. ..AND THE TWITTER TEST...AND THE YOU TUBE TEST...AND THE FACEBOOK TEST

Assume that anything you do will show up in the Newspaper and with all of the high-tech social networking applications very, very, very quickly. Twitter, U-Tube, Facebook, and other Social Networking sites reveal positive and negative experiences very quickly. How do you want the headline to read? You want good press and that comes from doing the right thing. The wrong thing does not just put you in the headlines and sell papers. It also has a chance of going viral and that can be very good or very bad! Good news spreads quickly, bad news spreads even faster. Make sure your organization understands the new communication reality.

AS THEY SAY IN ALCOHOLICS ANONYMOUS...PLACE PRINCIPLES BEFORE PERSONALITIES

If you manage by principle, the hard decisions become easy. It takes the individual out of the situation. The decision is the decision no matter who is involved. That prevents perceived favoritism to certain employees, resentful employees of your "favorites" and you, and potential legal action because you may have discriminated in your decision process. Keep your principles ahead of the personalities.

MEETING ATTENDANCE IS SUCCESSFUL IF YOU TAKE AWAY ONE GOOD IDEA

I view any meeting I attend to be successful if I take away at least one idea that makes me money, saves me time, or helps me in any way. Make sure you get that one good idea. It may not be from the actual meeting. It could be in the bar after the meeting or during the breaks while networking. Look for the one good idea. As the leader, make sure your people walk away with at least one good idea from your meetings as well.

IF YOU SLEEP WITH BIG DOGS YOU GET BIG FLEAS

If you sleep with big dogs, catching big fleas can't be avoided.   Do not partner with people or organizations that do not have solid core values. You will get fleas that will destroy you and your organization.

YOU ARE KNOWN BY THE COMPANY YOU KEEP

Your momma and your daddy used to tell you this and it is true. If you partner with a company, you will be known by their reputation. Make sure what they do will pass the Front Page Test.

NEVER ACCEPT A SALE OR ANY DEAL IF IT COMPROMISES YOUR VALUES

There can be no price on your values. They are worth much more to you over the long term than a short term gain will ever mean.

LOOK FOR THE VALUES WHEN HIRING SOMEONE

You need people who have the core values you need and want driving your organization. If you hire people with solid core values, they will make the right decisions without someone having to double check what they are doing. When the pressure is on and time is tight, you want the person with the solid values making decisions.

MAKE SURE POTENTIAL HIRES SPEND TIME WITH OTHERS IN YOUR ORGANIZATION

They will catch things you may not and the longer someone spends with you and your people, the more their true colors come out. Some people can interview well and pretend to be someone they are not for a while, but they can't fool all of the people all of the time.

IT IS WHAT YOU DO EVERYDAY THAT COUNTS

Success isn't just an event. It is a direct result of what we do and think everyday. There are no shortcuts or no major "aha" that thrusts success upon us. It is what we do everyday that counts and makes us successful.

YOU CAN LEARN A LOT ABOUT YOUR POTENTIAL HIRES BY THEIR QUESTIONS AND CONCERNS

If someone you are interviewing continually asks questions about the training program, they may be looking for you to make them successful. If they tell you they are concerned about making cold calls, you probably don't want to place them in sales.

USE YOUR POWER FOR GOOD AND NOT FOR EVIL

As a leader, your actions have an impact on others and you need to think about the consequences of your actions. What you do impacts your people, their families, stockholders, vendors and many others. Use your power for good and not for evil.

ALWAYS THINK WIN-WIN

Don't ever go to an "I win, you lose" approach with a customer or your colleagues. The people who lose will not want to do business with you again, nor will they want to help you when you need help. More than likely they will be determined to make sure you lose in the future. You may never even see it coming.

THE LONG TERM IMPLICATIONS OF YOUR DECISIONS ARE MORE IMPORTANT THAN THE SHORT TERM GAIN YOU MAY REALIZE

Always remember to think about the long term implications of a decision versus the vision and long term plan you have for your organization. A decision without weighing your long term plan may give you an immediate hit, but if long term it works against your vision, it is a wrong decision to make.

HAVING MANY YEARS OF EXPERIENCE IS NOT ALWAYS A GOOD THING

If the ten year veteran in your organization actually had the same one year of experience ten times, experience works against you rather than for you. Make sure your organization doesn't keep getting the same one year of experience over and over again.

NOT MAKING A DECISION IS MAKING A DECISION

When you procrastinate, the non-decision becomes your decision. Not making that decision is an action step so prepare for the consequences of putting off the decision.

STEALING IS STEALING IS STEALING

Padding an expense report is the same as going to the local convenience store and sticking your hand in the cash register and pulling out a handful of dollar bills. Stealing is Stealing even if you have a tie on and no gun in your hand.

WALK AWAY FROM BUSINESS THAT WILL NOT BE PROFITABLE FOR YOU OR FOR YOUR COMPANY

It always has to be a win-win for you and your company. If you are selling business that is not profitable, you will not have that company very long. Folks that look out for their companies first will always get better treatment from the folks who make decisions.

NO SQUARE PEGS IN ROUND HOLES

Too much time is wasted trying to place a square peg in a round hole. Walk away from business that will not fit your process or your operation. Manual processes that do not fit your business model can cost you a lot of money and produce an unhappy customer.

THE BEST LEADERS ARE THE BEST LISTENERS

They pay attention to what their employees, customers and vendors are telling them. They value their employees' opinions. They also realize that not listening can lead to miscommunications and an organization marching to many different drummers.

PEOPLE WHO DO NOT HAVE GOALS WILL ALWAYS WORK FOR THOSE WHO DO HAVE GOALS

People who have clear, specific, written goals will always accomplish more than those who don't have goals. Those people always rise to the top and above the folks who are just doing things everyday. As a result, those who don't have goals end up working for those who don't.

BE PASSIONATE ABOUT WHAT YOU DO AND ABOUT DOING THE RIGHT THING AT ALL TIMES

Your passion will be contagious. You will attract people who want to be with a leader who is excited about what they are doing and who can be counted on for doing the right thing no matter what the circumstance.

BE ENTHUSIASTIC AND ENERGETIC AT ALL TIMES!

Once again, you will attract people who want to be enthusiastic and energetic. They will want to help you, work with you, buy from you, and just be around you. Enthusiasm is contagious.

TAKE RESPONSIBILITY FOR THE RESULTS OF YOUR ORGANIZATION

Most companies reward people for attaining results and for owning the results of the organization. The best leaders own the results and make no excuses for failing to make results. Too many people try to avoid responsibility for their actions and ultimate results and just try to survive in an organization. Take responsibility and own the results and you will be rewarded.

ALWAYS CREDIT YOUR PEOPLE FOR THE GOOD THAT HAPPENS IN YOUR ORGANIZATION!

Effective leaders always give the credit for the good things to the people who made them happen. They realize the results they obtained would not have happened unless the people they work with did what they did.

NEVER BLAME YOUR PEOPLE FOR A LACK OF RESULTS OR A MISTAKE

Effective leaders never point the finger somewhere else. They always take responsibility for the things that went wrong.

LET THE LAW OF AVERAGES WORK FOR YOU

Leaders always know that you win by giving yourself as many opportunities to win as you can. Sales Leaders in any organization contests are almost always the ones who produced the most activity and made the most calls. They give themselves more opportunities to lose and to win. The law of averages will help you be successful if you give yourself enough opportunities.

ADAPT TO CHANGE QUICKLY AS CHANGE IS THE ONLY CONSTANT WE HAVE TODAY

Individuals and organizations that can not adapt to change are doomed to fail. Technological advances, globalization, and the merging of companies and cultures require that you be aware of changing circumstances and that you be prepared to react to them. Change can destroy your company or present opportunities for you to be successful. If you are not adaptable to change, you could lose everything. On the other hand, if you are adaptable to change you can not only survive, but can prosper given the new opportunities change can present.

THE BEST KNOWLEDGE COMES WHEN WE THINK WE KNOW IT ALL

Those that think that they know it all are in for a rude awakening. They leave themselves wide open for others to teach them the valuable lesson that they have not learned it all. Thinking you know it all creates a blind spot for you and prevents you from being open to new ideas or unable to recognize growing threats to your success. Never allow yourself or others you work with to have that "Know it all" attitude.

KNOWLEDGE IS NOTHING IF WE DON'T USE IT

It doesn't matter how much you know if you don't apply that knowledge. One can have the greatest sales presentation ever seen but it is worthless if you don't show it to enough people. The s ame is true with knowledge. It does n't matter how much knowledge we have if we just keep it in our heads. Use that knowledge for bettering the organization and yourself. Don't let it collect dust.

KNOWLEDGE IS NOTHING IF YOU CAN'T SHARE THAT KNOWLEDGE IN TERMS THAT EVERYONE CAN UNDERSTAND

Using big words does not help you if your audience doesn't understand the words. Your success in getting an idea across is how well your audience understands your message. It is up to you to adapt to your audience to get your message across. It is not up to the audience to change how they comprehend to understand your message. If people don't understand what you are saying they will not understand your vision and can't help you get there. Your customers will not understand what you are offering. Make sure you can convey your knowledge so that everyone can understand.

PROMOTE FROM WITHIN AS OFTEN AS POSSIBLE

The challenge is that we know all of the shortcomings of someone within the organization. We don't know the shortcomings of someone coming in from outside. We see their resume that is positioned to make the external candidate look good and not bad. No external candidate has ever given you a reference where the reference gave them a bad review. They could look better on paper than they actually are. We do know that if we don't promote from within, there will be resentment and distractions within the organization   We also know that the external candidate is going to have a burn-in period learning the organization and becoming self-sufficient in the organization. Unless there are specific skills that your people do not have, you are almost always better positioned if you promote from within. It sends the right message to your people and creates more loyalty in the organization. You also prevent bringing in perhaps some bad behavior and someone who can create turmoil. Promote from within as often as possible.

DO NOT DWELL ON WHAT YOU DON'T HAVE OR WHAT YOU CAN'T DO...FOCUS ON WHAT YOU DO HAVE AND WHAT YOU CAN DO

Too many people allow circumstance to dictate their success. If you don't have something or can't do something, you don't give up. You either figure out a way to get what you need or learn to do what you can't do, or you find ways to win without those things. Too much time is wasted thinking about why we can't do something as compared to taking action with what we can.

MANAGERS WHO MANAGE UP AS THEIR PRIMARY JOB SKILL CAN KILL YOUR BUSINESS

Many people can manage up very well and have made a career of managing up. People who put their primary focus on managing up and not managing and leading their people, managing across the organization, and paying attention to their external customers are dangerous to your organization. They can kill your business as they will run off good performers and customers and make it difficult for other departments to cooperate within the organization. The way to expose these folks is to not just have their boss do their performance reviews. Get the input of their employees, their associates, their internal customers and their external customers. That will give you a complete picture of their performance. Employee Surveys prior to implementation of 360 reviews had comments such as "If I could do my bosses review, he or she would never get another promotion." Make sure people are leading the organization and not just managing up by conducting 360 degree reviews. Having an organization with a multitude of folks whose primary goal is to manage up can kill your organization.

NUMBERS CAN HIDE WHAT IS REALLY GOING ON IN AN ORGANIZATION OR WITH PEOPLE

Make sure you don't assume that the fundamentals are ok just because the numbers are there. Sometimes the numbers can be from a large customer that you are too dependent upon and sometimes numbers can come because people are cheating or taking short cuts. They can also allow a bad leader to continue in the role to the detriment of your people and your organization.

WHERE THERE IS SMOKE THERE IS USUALLY A FIRE

If you are hearing rumors about someone or some department's business practices that could be inappropriate and harmful to your organization, you should dig around a bit. Chances are good something is going on. When you do investigate, pay attention to the reaction. If you sense a "stiff arm" that is an attempt to keep you from gathering the facts or a "closing of the ranks" when you start questioning, by all means, dig even deeper.

RECOGNIZE YOU INITIALLY ONLY SEE THE TIP OF THE ICEBERG

If you know about a few issues that concern you about a person's behaviour, you need to recognize that you are only seeing the tip of the iceberg. The issues are usually much larger. Once the person is gone, you will see the entire iceberg. All of the issues will expose themselves.

FEAR AND INTIMIDATION AS A MOTIVATOR LAST ONLY A SHORT TIME

Many leaders think the only way to get better performance is to have people intimidated and afraid. The boss is in charge and in control. This environment is stressful and not a fun place to work. Growth is stifled and people will do what they need to do to survive but they will either leave or do their best to undermine the boss. Fear and Intimidation can provide short term productivity hits but never last and help an organization grow to be the best it can be.

SPEAK TO EVERYONE YOU SEE EACH DAY

If you are the boss your people may think they have done something wrong if you ignore them. They immediately think the worst. "Wonder what I did to tick the boss off?" Speak to everyone. You will be amazed at the loyalty you build and the performance you attain.

REMEMBER, TREATING PEOPLE POORLY ON THE WAY UP INSURES THAT YOU WILL FIND THE WAY DOWN QUICKLY

Treat everyone you meet with respect as you rise to the top. If you do, people will help you get to the top. If you don't, they will make sure you get a chance to see them again on your way down and they will do their best to hasten your fall.

GOOD LEADERS DO NOT LET THEIR WEAK POINTS GET IN THE WAY OF THEIR STRENGTHS

No one can do it all and know it all in this day and age. We all have things we don't do particularly well. On the other hands, there are things we do that are outstanding. Work from your strengths while minimizing your weaknesses.

LACK OF TRUST IN YOUR PEOPLE CAN DESTROY YOUR ORGANIZATION

Lack of trust drives too many rules and sign-offs that slows your organization down and costs money to administer. Your people will grow weary of the lack of trust and will leave the organization. Turnover of the wrong people always hurts.

TRUST AND FAIRNESS STILL MEAN SOMETHING

Trust and a reputation for being fair is a differential for you in attracting and retaining employees and customers. People still want to trust and to know that fairness still means something. Your organization can accomplish greatness by being trustworthy and fair.

WE CAN BE TOO BUSY TO MAKE MONEY

Organizations and people can allow themselves to get so busy that they can't make money. They are so busy doing the day-to-day minor things that they think are major that they can lose sight of how they make money. An example is too many "FYI Keep people in the loop" conference calls or meetings. We can do so many of those that all of our time is spent doing that as opposed to making money. We can be too busy to make money.

CREATE A LEADERSHIP SUCCESSION PROGRAM

Good Leaders develop their replacements and make sure that replacement planning occurs throughout the organization. A mark of a well run, well developed organization is that it can sustain itself when leaders depart.

LEADERS TAKE PEOPLE BEYOND THE ORDINARY

Your role as a leader is to influence others to go beyond what they thought was possible. Your role is to take them beyond the ordinary.

NEVER APOPOGIZE FOR EXPECTING EXCELLENT RESULTS FROM YOUR ORGANIZATION AND ITS PEOPLE

We receive what we expect and while there may be some who feel you are asking too much sometimes, if the leader doesn't have high expectations, no one else will.

BE SMART ENOUGH TO HIRE
PEOPLE SMARTER THAN YOU ARE

The best leaders always make sure they get their ego's out of the way and hire people who may be smarter than they are. They are not afraid to have people who are smarter than they are working with them. The results will speak for themselves.

DON'T CONFUSE JUST FIGHTING FOR YOUR PEOPLE AS BEING THE MARK OF A GOOD LEADER

Fighting for your people when the fight is for a cause or decision that is bad for your business prevents you from being a good leader!
Fighting for your people is important, but a good leader knows when winning the fight for your people would have a long term negative implication for the business.   That ultimately has a negative impact on the people.

A MAJOR FACTOR IN BEING A GOOD LEADER IS JUST SHOWING UP

You can't lead an organization if you are not there. You have to show up. You have to be visible. You need to be a part of what is going on. Your people need to know you are there and where you want them to take the organization.

KNOW WHEN TO ASK FOR ADVICE

The best leaders recognize they don't know everything and know when to ask for advice. They will have people they trust to give them advice when they are outside of their comfort zone or expertise.

BE WILLING TO TAKE AN UNPOPULAR STAND WHEN IT IS THE RIGHT THING TO DO

It takes courage to go against the grain and to take an unpopular stand. That courage is necessary to make sure your organization does the right thing. You are not there to be most popular; you are there to get results the right way and to take the organization to a higher level.

THERE IS NEVER A REASON TO DO A WRONG THING

Doing the wrong thing is never right. No disguise or spin or justification can make a wrong thing to do the right thing to do. If it is wrong, don't do it.

ARROGANCE IS YOUR ENEMY

Arrogance has brought down many leaders who were originally seen as getting the job done! They start believing their press clippings and think they are invincible. Arrogance prevents you from seeing what is really happening. Arrogance will also keep you from listening to advice that can keep you and your organization out of trouble.

DON'T CONFUSE ARROGANCE WITH CONFIDENCE

It is one thing to be confident but if taken to the extreme, it becomes arrogance and that can lead to blindness for you and your organization. We can make ourselves deny that we are arrogant in our delusion that we are just being self-confident.

IF HIGH PAYING JOBS WERE EASY, THEY WOULDN'T BE HIGH PAYING JOBS!

If your job is easy and without mental challenges and stress, not only will you not grow, you are not going to make a lot of money. The reasons some jobs yield more money is because there is a higher level of challenge, stress and risk. Anyone can do the easy job so the law of supply and demand takes over. You can find a lot of people to do the easy job. You can't find a lot of people who can perform the more challenging roles and they are in greater demand. As a result, they make more money. High paying jobs only become easy because people have the passion and the desire to do those jobs. They love it and thrive in that environment.

YOUR GREATEST STRENGTH CAN ALSO BE YOUR GREATEST WEAKNESS

Having a high regard for people can be your strength, but it can be a weakness if it prevents you from dealing with performance issues. Your strategic thought process can be your strength but can also be a weakness if too much time is spent strategizing and not enough time executing. The key is to make sure you don't allow your strengths to become weaknesses.

ASK APPLICANTS FOR THEIR EXPECTATIONS OF THEIR MANAGERS

In interviews applicants will tell you what they want in their manager or leader if you ask them. The overwhelming majority want a leader who is clear with their expectations and lets them do the job but is there when they need them. If they indicate they want their manager to show them what to do all of the time or spend too much time talking about the training the manager should do, you should probably look for another candidate. They are looking for others to make them successful.

DON'T MAJOR IN THE MINORS

Too many managers major in the minors. They focus on the small items and not the high pay-off initiatives. Major in the majors not the minors.

PEOPLE HAVE TO WANT TO CHANGE TO CHANGE

Good leaders recognize that they can't change others! They know that they can only change themselves. They can influence others to change themselves by creating the climate for change.

AS IN GOLF, TENNIS, AND ALL SPORTS, FOLLOW-THROUGH IS KEY

The best strategy in the world is worthless if there is no follow through. You will only hit the ball halfway if you don't follow-through in golf or tennis or any other sport. The same is true in business. No follow-through means a missed opportunity.

DON'T LET YOUR GOALS GATHER DUST

Don't write out your goals and then set them on a shelf. Place them where you can see them everyday. Place them in your car, in your bathroom, on your wall, on your refrigerator. You need to see them frequently everyday. You will accomplish your goals if you are reminded of them.

CARVE OUT CREATIVE TIME

Don't allow the urgent day-to-day keep you from creating new ideas or better ways to accomplish your goals. Step away from the fray and spend time thinking about your business and how you can generate more or do things better. The day-to-day can kill your imagination if you don't schedule the time for creativity.

IN THE ABSENCE OF GOOD LEADERSHIP, THE ORGANIZATION WILL FIND THEIR LEADERS

If you want to insure that your organization will be successful, lead the organization. Don't allow the organization to follow leaders that may have interests counter to the organization's best long term interests.

ADVERSITY WILL LET YOU SEE EVERYONE'S TRUE CHARACTER

When tough times hit, you have an opportunity to reveal who you truly are. The values and principles that guide you day to day will be exposed. Look at adversity as an opportunity to demonstrate who you are and how you deal with difficult issues. Observing how others deal with adversity allows you to see who they really are and what values they may or may not possess.

RESTRUCTURING YOUR ORGANIZATION REQUIRES TOUGH PEOPLE DECISIONS

Restructuring can be a good idea to operate more effectively, but if you are reorganizing due to poor performers in key roles, placing those key players in the restructured organization will just bring more poor performance. Restructuring will usually work best when you place different players in the line-up. Many times the issue isn't how you are structured; it is the performance of key individuals.   Unfortunately, many organization leaders avoid conflict and dealing with poor performance by restructuring. Deal with the performance for best results.

NO ONE IS BIGGER THAN THE SYSTEM

Good leaders realize that no one is bigger than the system. People who cheat, steal and try to beat the system are in many cases highly talented and creative people who think that the rules are meant for someone else. No matter what happens they will feel that their position was the right one and they will never admit that they did anything wrong. If you let one of these individuals continue in your organization, you are going to have issues. You will have issues with your other associates, your customers, your stakeholders, and you may find yourself in the newspaper, and not in a good way, or defending your organization in legal actions. You can not let anyone be bigger than your system.

ARROGANCE IS A LEADING CAUSE OF FAILURE FOR COMPANIES AND INDIVIDUALS ALIKE

Arrogance keeps you from seeing what the competition is doing. It prevents you from seeing external and internal trends developing that will have an impact on your business or your profession. You don't think you need to worry about anything or anyone else. It also may put you in a position where your organization doesn't think that the rules pertain to them. You do not see the world nor your own business or organization clearly. You simply don't think you can be beat but arrogance is different than self-confidence. Arrogance will make you miss opportunities and will allow others to overtake you.

HONESTY IS NOT GREY

There is no grey area in Honesty. Either you are or you are not. Either you did it honestly or you did not. There is no grey in Honesty.

DON'T REACH DOWN TO PICK UP A PENNY IF IT MEANS A FIFTY DOLLAR BILL FALLS OUT OF YOUR POCKET

We have all seen people who do this. They are so excited that they have found a penny that they don't notice $50 falling out of their pocket. Don't focus on the pennies. Focus on the Fifties.

PROCRASTINATION CAN BURY YOU

Procrastinating with a problem will only make the problem become larger. The problem grows worse, the potential solutions disappear, and the next thing you know, the problem has buried you. Deal with problems and issues right away. Very rarely does procrastinating have a positive outcome.

COMPENSATION PLANS SHOULD ALIGN WITH OBJECTIVES

The best run companies align their compensation plans with the objectives of the business. That way, if your people are making money, the company is making money. No one from Finance will resent the large commissions paid to a Sales Rep or a Sales Manager if the compensation is aligned with the profits of the organization and their bonus plans.

COMPENSATION PLANS MUST ALIGN THROUGHOUT THE ORGANIZATION

Your compensation plans should mirror each other up and down the organization. If your boss is paid based on the same activities and results, you don't have to worry that he or she has a different agenda when making decisions. Pay everyone based on the same objectives.

JUMP AND THEN GROW WINGS

Sometimes you can't be totally prepared and you can't wait for your wings to grow. Sometimes you have to make the jump and have faith you will grow wings. Have faith in yourself and your abilities.

TRUST IS NOT AN ENTITLEMENT

Trust of the leader by the people in the organization isn't automatically bestowed on the leader. It is earned by your actions day in and day out. Do what you say you are going to do. Walk the talk. Be genuine and always shoot straight with your people.

TRUST YOUR EMPLOYEES IN HIRING NEW PEOPLE FOR YOUR TEAM

Your employees will be able to see things you can't. They will see how the individual will fit in. They will be committed to helping that person be successful since they recommended them.

YOUR PERKS BELONG TO YOUR EMPLOYEES

Rank does have privileges but it can be costly to your organization's morale. For example, if you have three covered parking spaces in Phoenix, Arizona, let your staff have those slots. Don't hog them. When it is 115 degrees and the staff realizes you are getting into a hot car and their car has been shaded all day, they will appreciate it. If you hog those because you are entitled to them, you will not earn their respect. If there are only x number of free parking spots, give them to the lowest paid employees first. It will mean a lot more to them financially than it will to you or your high paid sales folks. Anyway, the high paid sales folks should be out selling and not in the office. They should not need the free parking.

BAD BOSSES ARE THE REASON YOUR PEOPLE QUIT

The departing employee may say they are leaving due to money or a better opportunity, but in reality, two-thirds of the time it is because they can't bear to work for their boss. Let your people do performance reviews on their boss. Eliminate the bad bosses and your employees will stay.

ELIMINATE THE INFORMATION FILTERS WITH SKIP LEVEL DISCUSSIONS

We need to realize that we can have people in our organizations who manage up well and keep their people in check so that the real information does not get to you. You need to make sure that your people are heard and a process where the levels below your direct reports have a safe and secure access to share information with you, will accomplish that. Skip levels to eliminate the filters.

EXCEPTIONS CAN BE HAZARDOUS TO YOUR ORGANIZATION'S HEALTH
Part 1.

We see it all of the time... you need to make an exception for a key customer and it goes against your model and requires extra expense and a manual process. That one decision on its own can make sense and seem like the right thing to do, but once you make a couple of hundred of those exceptions, you have chaos in your operations. You make mistakes and you have unhappy customers and unhappy employees. Chaos comes from a couple of hundred good individual decisions on exceptions.

EXCEPTIONS CAN BE HAZARDOUS TO YOUR ORGANIZATIONS HEALTH, PART 2.

Make an exception for one employee and you better be prepared to make the exceptions for all of the other employees needing an exception for the same circumstance. If you don't you are no longer being consistent and fair and you will have a demoralized organization. Be consistent and avoid exceptions unless you are willing to make that same decision for everyone.

BURY YOUR DEAD

Too many organizations simply reorganize and move their performance issues to different jobs in the organization. When Leaders do that, they are taking an expedient approach and fostering mediocrity. They don't want to go through the coaching, performance warning process, and then have to tell someone they are fired. They are taking a shortcut. Most of the time the performance problem will not only be a performance issue in their new role, they will also be angry and resentful to you and to the organization. If they get a chance to discredit you, they will. Most of the time you will have left an enemy in the organization whose primary motivation is to get back at you. If you have fired them, they can not bring you or your organization down. Bury your dead. Don't let them come back to life.

IF WHAT YOU DID YESTERDAY STILL LOOKS BIG TODAY, YOU HAVEN'T ACCOMPLISHED MUCH TODAY

Looking in the rear view mirror will not help you drive forward. You have to have your eyes on the road ahead. Celebrate your accomplishments and be proud of them but don't waste your time thinking that accomplishment is enough to carry you.

LAURELS GROW THIN

When you rest on those Laurels, they grow thin. Keep trying to beat what you did yesterday, everyday!

STRIKE WHEN HOT

When you accomplish something, make a big sale, negotiate a deal, etc., take action to continue the momentum. Strike while you are hot. The best time to make another sale is when you are feeling good about a sale you just made. You see it over and over again in sports. A team gets hot and they just continue to stay hot. They have the momentum and they attack to keep that momentum going. Do the same in business. Strike when you are hot.

AVOIDING ADDING LAYERS OF MANAGEMENT SHOULD BE EQUAL TO AVOIDING THE PLAGUE

Too many levels of management means you have too many people who will make work for the rest of the organization. Too many times the work that is added is not adding value. It adds to the bureaucracy and the frustration levels of your associates who actually do the work. It adds to your overhead and the extra levels slow you down. They also seem to filter information coming to you so that you may not get an accurate read on what is actually happening. Avoid adding layers of management like you avoid the plague.

THE EMPLOYEES CLOSEST TO THE CUSTOMERS ARE TRULY THE ONES YOU CAN LEAST AFFORD TO LOSE

If you have to cut some employees just for an expense reduction, it should always start with the levels that operate the most distance from the customer. Don't disrupt the customer relationships if they are going good. Look for the true overhead to cut.

AVOID THE "IT WORKED SO WELL WE STOPPED DOING IT" PHENOMENON

Too many times there are things that worked so well, we stopped doing it. They may be the little things that we take for granted that have helped us be successful, such as Thank you notes, proactive calls to happy customers, etc. They worked but somehow they get lost in the shuffle until we suddenly realize that it worked so well we stopped doing it.

GREAT LEADERSHIP IS SIMPLE

Great Leadership is simple. It is truly exercising common sense, caring, communicating, respecting everyone, expecting amazing results and always doing the right thing.

TOO MANY ROUND TUITS WILL CREATE PROBLEMS

Don't allow the Round Tuits to stack up. You know those Round Tuits. You say One day I will get Round Tuit on something. Make sure you don't have too many of those Round Tuits. They will kill you.

DON'T HIRE SPRINTERS IF YOUR BUSINESS NEEDS MARATHONERS

Match your hires with your business needs. Know what attributes your employees and the various positions need and hire those people.

IF IT IS RAINING, LOOK FOR THE RAINBOW

When you are experiencing bad times, Leaders need to reinforce that there is still a Rainbow coming. People need to know that things will change and you can't see the Rainbow unless there has been Rain.

DO NOT DEVELOP PARALYSIS OVER ANALYSIS

Guard against over-thinking a situation. Sometimes folks spend so much time analyzing a situation they miss the opportunity.

SUCCESSFUL LEADERS DO THE THINGS UNSUCCESSFUL LEADERS DON'T WANT TO DO

Successful Leaders ask for candid feedback and advice. They listen to what is really happening and not just what they want to hear. They take action as a result of what they hear. They also address performance issues by terminating those individuals if a behaviour change can't be accomplished. They don't just reassign problem employees. They eliminate barriers their employees face in completing their missions. They roll up their sleeves and take action.

TRUST IS A MUST

Leaders must be seen as someone that can be trusted. If the leader is trusted, their people will perform to their best of their abilities. If the leader is not trusted, they will spend their time trying to figure out what the leader is up to, and less time achieving the organization's goals. They will undermine the leader. When trust goes away, it takes with it productivity and profit. Remember that Trust is not an entitlement. It has to be earned every day by the leader. Trust is a must. That isn't just for the Leader's people. Customers, vendors, and other stake holders have to be able to trust the Leader. If there is no trust, ultimately, there is no business. Trust is a must.

HOGS GET SLAUGHTERED

As the Leader you can not get greedy. If you hog all of the glory, all of the money, and all of the benefits, your people will resent you and undermine you. Greed gets in the way of being a Great Leader. Greed can make you develop blind spots. Hogs get slaughtered in the end. Don't be a hog.

GREAT LEADERS EXPECT THEIR PEOPLE TO ASK FOR FORGIVENESS RATHER THAN FOR PERMISSION

Great Leaders should want an organization that acts and takes risks. Leaders don't want an organization where your people have to ask permission to take action or to take care of customers. If the Leader has communicated the vision and the expectations, you want your people to feel they can ask for forgiveness if they make a mistake rather than have to wait for permission to do something because they fear the consequences of a mistake. Create the environment where people ask for forgiveness rather than permission to take action.

NEGATIVE ENERGY IS JUST AS CONTAGIOUS AS ENTHUSIASM

People with negative attitudes create negative energy. Do not allow those folks to stay in your organization. They will drain the enthusiasm and the positive energy that you need to be successful.   It is ok to have people who disagree or question as you need that to make sure you are headed in the right direction. However, there is a big difference between questioning and disagreeing and folks who are just negative in general and really can't be on board with where you are headed.

THE TORTOISE WILL ALWAYS BEAT THE HARE OVER THE LONG TERM!

While the Hare might win the short term race, the Tortoise will methodically outlast the Hare over time. Steady advancement might not always be the most exciting to watch, but when the Hare has been caught by the Coyote or hit by the car as the Hare crosses the road, the Tortoise is still plodding along waiting for the next Hare that will come to challenge the Tortoise.

ETHICS ARE NOT MADE OF ELASTIC OR PLAY DOUGH

Ethics don't stretch with the times like elastic belts or melded like play dough for the situation.

SO HARD TO BUILD, SO EASY TO DESTROY

It is incredibly difficult to build a successful world class organization, yet so easy to destroy it. Just put a bad leader in charge and you can quickly destroy what it took, in many circumstances, years to build.

TOO MUCH INTERNAL FOCUS IS A CANCER THAT MUST BE ELIMINATED

Too many companies allow a bureaucracy to grow that will force more internal focus than external focus. It is like a cancer spreading through out your organization. If you have executives who spend more than half of their time participating in internal conference calls and meetings every week, when are they going to have time to be out with the customers? If your people are tied up on internal issues, you are headed for trouble. If you find in your planning process that the obstacles and threats that are identified as potentially preventing you from attaining your goals are more internal than external, you have to take quick action as your organization is tied up in its own issues.

AS THE CARTOON CHARACTER POGO ONCE SAID, I HAVE SEEN THE ENEMY AND IT IS US

Too many times our obstacles are internal rather than external.   If your organization is its own worst enemy, you need to really listen to your front-line folks to find out what they need to serve the customer.

ABOUT THE AUTHOR

D. Lane Stephens has spent 37 years in the insurance business and has been managing and leading Sales Organizations for over 30 of those years. His leadership practices and theories go beyond the insurance business and apply to anyone in a leadership role. Lane and his wife Michele live in Paradise Valley, Arizona. They have three children, one daughter-in-law and one granddaughter. Lane and Michele also have two labs, a chocolate one and a yellow one, who have trained Lane very well.